HAL•LEONARD

INSTRUMENTAL PLAY-ALONG

AUDIO ACCESS INCLUDED

PLAYBACK+
Speed • Pitch • Balance • Loop

FLUTE

Disney MARY POPPINS RETURNS

MUSIC BY MARC
LYRICS BY SCOTT WITTMAN   AN

Audio Arrangements by Peter Deneff

To access audio, visit:
www.halleonard.com/mylibrary

Enter Code
8647-2511-7406-1117

ISBN 978-1-5400-4585-0

HAL•LEONARD®

Visit Hal Leonard Online at
www.halleonard.com

Contact us:
Hal Leonard
7777 West Bluemound Road
Milwaukee, WI 53213
Email: info@halleonard.com

In Europe, contact:
Hal Leonard Europe Limited
42 Wigmore Street
Marylebone, London, W1U 2RN
Email: info@halleonardeurope.com

In Australia, contact:
Hal Leonard Australia Pty. Ltd.
4 Lentara Court
Cheltenham, Victoria, 3192 Australia
Email: info@halleonard.com.au

CAN YOU IMAGINE THAT?

FLUTE

Music by MARC SHAIMAN
Lyrics by SCOTT WITTMAN and MARC SHAIMAN

A CONVERSATION

FLUTE

Music by MARC SHAIMAN
Lyrics by SCOTT WITTMAN and MARC SHAIMAN

A COVER IS NOT THE BOOK

Flute

Music by MARC SHAIMAN
Lyrics by SCOTT WITTMAN and MARC SHAIMAN

(Underneath the)
LOVELY LONDON SKY

FLUTE

Music by MARC SHAIMAN
Lyrics by SCOTT WITTMAN and MARC SHAIMAN

NOWHERE TO GO BUT UP

FLUTE

Music by MARC SHAIMAN
Lyrics by SCOTT WITTMAN and MARC SHAIMAN

THE PLACE WHERE LOST THINGS GO

FLUTE

Music by MARC SHAIMAN
Lyrics by SCOTT WITTMAN and MARC SHAIMAN

THE ROYAL DOULTON MUSIC HALL

FLUTE

Music by MARC SHAIMAN
Lyrics by SCOTT WITTMAN and MARC SHAIMAN

TRIP A LITTLE LIGHT FANTASTIC

FLUTE

Music by MARC SHAIMAN
Lyrics by SCOTT WITTMAN and MARC SHAIMAN

TURNING TURTLE

FLUTE

Music by MARC SHAIMAN
Lyrics by SCOTT WITTMAN and MARC SHAIMAN

Fast Broadway 2